cute little

10 CONTEMPORARY HANDKNITS FOR

Jem Weston

PHOTOGRAPHY BY Steven Wooster

ROWAN

Cute Little Knits
First published in 2012 by
Rowan Yarns
Green Lane Mill
Holmfirth
HD9 2DX

Created and produced by
Berry & Co (Publishing) Ltd
47 Crewys Road, Childs Hill
London NW2 2AU

Design Anne Wilson
Pattern editing/charts Lisa Richardson
Editor Katie Hardwicke
Additional photography Rosie McPherson pp 18, 19, 52,
cover (back, bottom left)

British LIbrary Cataloguing in Publication Data
A catalogue record of this book is available from the
British Library

ISBN 978-1-907544-40-8
Printed in Singapore

Contents

Lovebirds cushion 4

Tile cushion 12

Chunky monkey 16

Lazy lace throw 24

Leaf hottie cover 28

Bobble bath mat 34

Bow slippers 38

Little hearts 42

Fantastic fox 48

Birdie cosies 54

KNITTING KNOW-HOW 61

YARN INFORMATION 63

SUPPLIERS 64

ACKNOWLEDGEMENTS 64

lovebirds cushion

This cushion, with its pair of lovebirds, has all the hallmarks of pared-down Japanese design with the birds positioned off-centre on a delicate branch. The tiny touch of contrasting colour for the beaks and feet of the birds could be knitted in a bright orange, yellow or pink, as you prefer. This cushion looks good paired with the Tile cushion (see pages 10–15).

Skill level
**

Finished size
Knitted cushion front measures approx 46cm/18in square

Yarns
Rowan *Wool Cotton*
A 2 x 50g/1½oz balls teal blue
    (968 Cypress)
B 1 x 50g/1½oz ball navy (909 French Navy)
C 1 x 50g/1½oz ball cream (900 Antique)
D 1 x 50g/1½oz ball light brown (965 Mocha)
E 1 x 50g/1½oz ball orange (985 Cafe)

Needles
1 pair 4mm (US size 6) needles

Extras
For both slip and buttoned fabric cushion back (as shown on page 15):
Two x 49 x 35cm/19¼ x 13¾in pieces of Denyse Schmidt Posie fabric in turquoise
46cm/18in square cushion pad
For buttoned version only:
Five x 22mm/¾in buttons (Coats 517)

Tension

22 sts and 30 rows to 10cm/4in square measured over St st using 4mm (US size 6) needles.

Abbreviations

See page 62.

Pattern notes

When working from chart, odd numbered rows are k rows and read from right to left. Even numbered rows are p rows and read from left to right.

This pattern uses both the Fairisle and intarsia method of joining colours (see page 61).

Front

Using yarn A and 4mm (US size 6) needles, cast on 103 sts.

Starting with a k row, work in St st for 30 rows, ending with a WS row.

Place chart

Cont in St st working 63 rows from chart using the Fairisle and intarsia techniques (Fairisle technique for birds' feet only), ending with a RS row.

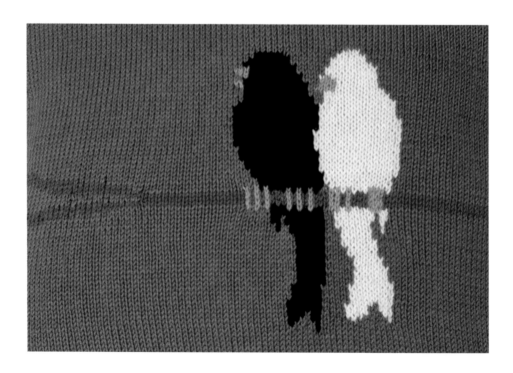

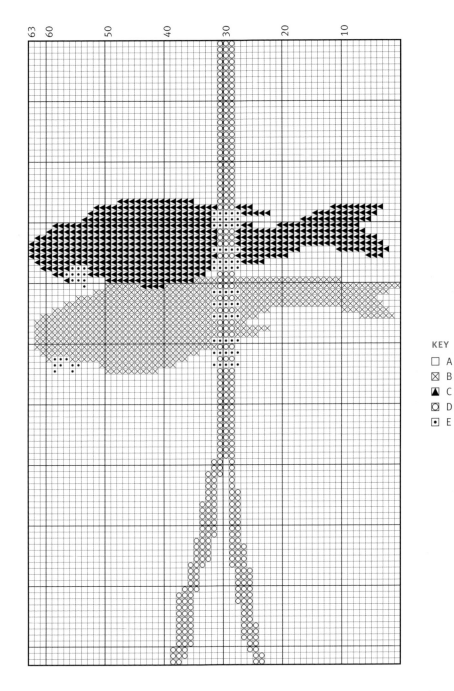

KEY

☐ A
☒ B
▲ C
◪ D
⊡ E

Cont in St st using yarn A only until front measures 46cm/18in, ending with a WS row. Cast off.

Making up

Cushion cover back – slip version
Overlock or zigzag stitch along all raw edges of fabric back panels. Turn under 2cm/¾in along one long edge of each piece and straight stitch in place. With the two pieces of fabric overlapping at the centre, pin and handstitch the two pieces to the knitted front.
Turn right sides out, insert cushion pad.

Cushion cover back – buttoned version
Overlock or zigzig stitch along all edges of fabric back panels. Turn under 2cm/¾in along one long edge of RH piece and straight stitch in place. Turn under 5cm/2in along one long edge of LH piece and straight stitch in place approx 4cm/1½in from edge creating the button band. Make 5 buttonholes evenly across button band starting approx 2.5cm/1in from top and bottom. Sew 5 buttons on RH piece in line with buttonholes. Overlap two pieces of fabric at the centre. Pin and handstitch to knitted front.
Turn right sides out, insert cushion pad.

Jem says
I think the lovebirds would look equally good knitted in white on a black background, with a green branch and bright red beaks and feet, or try a monochrome version in shades of grey, with pink beaks and feet.

tile cushion

This elegant cushion was inspired by antique blue-and-white ceramic tiles.
Swapping a couple of the blue designs for an orange and brown one adds a
contemporary twist.

cute little knits

Skill level
**

Finished size
Knitted cushion front measures approx 46cm/18in square

Yarns
Rowan *Wool Cotton*
A 2 x 50g/1½oz balls cream (900 Antique)
B 1 x 50g/1½oz ball teal blue
      (968 Cypress)
C 1 x 50g/1½oz ball orange (985 Cafe)
D 1 x 50g/1½oz ball light brown
      (965 Mocha)

Needles
1 pair 4mm (US size 6) needles

Extras
For both slip and buttoned fabric cushion back (as shown on page 15):
Two x 49 x 35cm/19¼ x 13¾in pieces of Denyse Schmidt Posie fabric in turquoise
46cm/18in square cushion pad
For buttoned version only:
Five x 22mm/¾in buttons (Coats 517)

Tension
22 sts and 30 rows to 10cm/4in square measured over St st using 4mm (US size 6) needles.

Abbreviations
See page 62.

Pattern notes
When working from chart, odd numbered rows are k rows and read from right to left. Even numbered rows are p rows and read from left to right.
This pattern uses the intarsia method of joining colours (see page 61).

Front
Using yarn A and 4mm (US size 6) needles, cast on 103 sts.
Working in St st throughout starting with a k row, complete 139 rows from chart on page 14.
Cast off.

Making up
Press as described on the information page (see page 62).

Cushion cover back – slip version
Overlock or zigzag stitch along all raw edges of fabric back panels. Turn under 2cm/¾in along one long edge of each piece and straight stitch in place. With the two pieces of fabric overlapping at the centre, pin and handstitch the two pieces to the knitted front.
Turn right sides out, insert cushion pad.

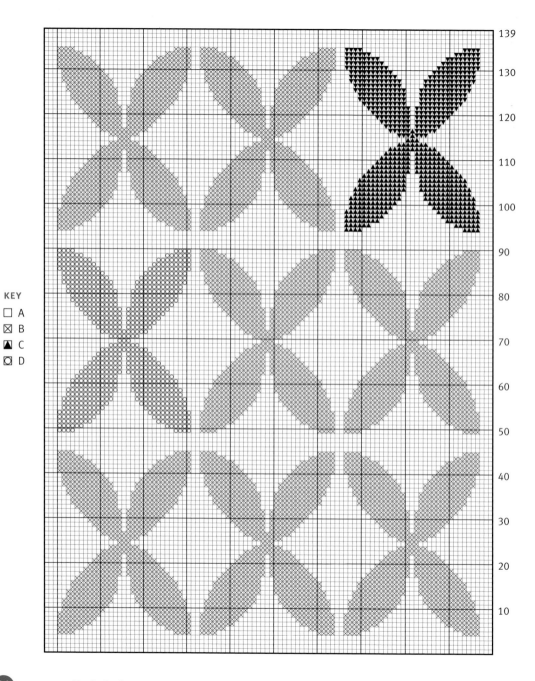

KEY
☐ A
☒ B
▲ C
◧ D

139
130
120
110
100
90
80
70
60
50
40
30
20
10

cute little knits

Cushion cover back – buttoned version

Overlock or zigzig stitch along all edges of fabric back panels. Turn under 2cm/¾in along one long edge of RH piece and straight stitch in place. Turn under 5cm/2in along one long edge of LH piece and straight stitch in place approx 4cm/1½in from edge creating the button band. Make 5 buttonholes evenly across button band starting approx 2.5cm/1in from top and bottom. Sew 5 buttons on RH piece in line with buttonholes. Overlap two pieces of fabric at centre. Pin and handstitch to the knitted front.

Turn right sides out, insert cushion pad.

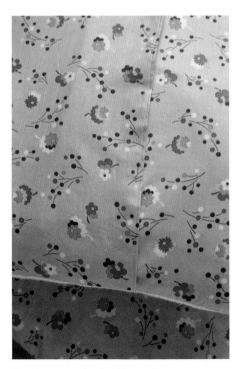

Cushion cover back: slip version

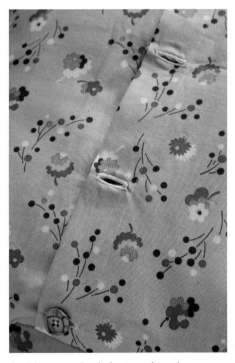

Cushion cover back: buttoned version

chunky monkey

Knitted in brown and beige Rowan *Felted Tweed DK*, this retro-style monkey comes with a choice of scarves (see pages 22–3) to give him a bit of a dash: a plain moss stitch one, a two-colour striped garter stitch one and a three-colour Fairisle version in stocking stitch.

Skill level
**

Finished size
Completed monkey is approx 49cm/19in tall x 35cm/14in wide

Yarns
For monkey only: Rowan *Felted Tweed DK*
A   2 x 50g/1½oz balls brown
     (153 Phantom)
B   1 x 50g/1½oz ball light brown
     (157 Camel)

Needles
1 pair 3.75mm (US size 5) needles
1 pair 2.75mm (US size 2) needles

Extras
Washable toy stuffing

Tension
23 sts and 32 rows to 10cm/4in square measured over St st using 3.75mm (US size 5) needles.

Abbreviations
See page 62.

Back
Using yarn A and 3.75mm (US size 5) needles, cast on 16 sts.
Row 1 Purl.
Row 2 K1, M1, k to last st, M1, k1. *18 sts*
Inc as set by Row 2 on 4 foll alt rows and 4 foll 4th rows. *34 sts*
Beg with p row, work 7 rows in St st.
Row 34 K1, k2tog, k to last 3 sts, k2tog tbl, k1. *32 sts*
Dec as set by Row 34 on foll 4th row and 6 foll alt rows. *18 sts*

Row 51 Purl.

Row 52 K to end, turn and cast on 7 sts.

25 sts

Row 53 P to end, turn and cast on 7 sts.

32 sts

Row 54 K to end, turn and cast on 34 sts.

66 sts

Row 55 P to end, turn and cast on 34 sts.

100 sts

Row 56 K34, k2tog, k28, k2tog tbl, k34.

98 sts

Purl next and every foll alt row.

Row 58 K33, k2tog, k28, k2tog tbl, k33.

96 sts

Row 60 K32, k2tog, k28, k2tog tbl, k32.

94 sts

Row 62 K31, k2tog, k28, k2tog tbl, k31.

92 sts

Row 64 K30, k2tog, k28, k2tog tbl, k30.

90 sts

Row 66 K29, k2tog, k28, k2tog tbl, k29.

88 sts

Row 68 K28, k2tog, k28, k2tog tbl, k28.

86 sts

Row 69 P27, p2tog, p28, p2tog tbl, p27.

84 sts

Row 70 Cast off 29 sts (1 st on right needle), k25.

Cast off rem 29 sts. *26 sts*

Rejoin yarn and work across these 26 sts.

**Beg with p row, work 9 rows in St st.
Row 80 K1, M1, k to last st, M1, k1. *28 sts*
Beg with p row, work 5 rows in St st.
Row 86 K1, M1, k to last st, M1, k1. *30 sts*
Inc as set by Row 86, on 3 foll 4th rows.
36 sts
Beg with p row, work 3 rows in St st.
Row 102 K1, k2tog, k to last 3 sts, k2tog tbl,
k1. *34 sts*
Beg with p row, work 5 rows in St st.
Row 108 K1, k2tog, k to last 3 sts, k2tog tbl,
k1. *32 sts*
Dec as set by Row 108, on 2 foll 4th rows.
28 sts
***Next row Purl.

Next row K14, turn leaving rem sts on holder.
Beg with p row, work 41 rows in St st.
Change to yarn B.
Next row K1, M1, k to last st, M1, k1. *16 sts*
Beg with p row, work 13 rows in St st.
Next row K1, k2tog, k to last 3 sts, k2tog tbl,
k1. *14 sts*
Dec as set on foll alt row. *12 sts*
Next row Purl.
Cast off.
With RS facing, rejoin yarn A to rem 14 sts.
Beg with k row, work 42 rows in St st.
Change to yarn B.
Next row K1, M1, k to last st, M1, k1. *16 sts*
Beg with p row, work 13 rows in St st.

Next row K1, k2tog, k to last 3 sts, k2tog tbl, k1. *14 sts*

Dec as set on foll alt row. *12 sts*

Next row Purl.

Cast off.

Front

Work as given for back to **.

Row 1 Purl.

Row 2 K10, M1, k to last 10 sts, M1, k10. *28 sts*

Inc as set by Row 2, on 7 foll alt rows and 4 foll 4th rows. *50 sts*

Beg with p row, work 3 rows in St st.

Row 36 K1, k2tog, k to last 3 sts, k2tog tbl, k1. *48 sts*

Purl next and every alt foll row.

Row 38 K1, k2tog, k10, k2tog, k18, k2tog tbl, k10, k2tog tbl, k1. *44 sts*

Row 40 K1, k2tog, k9, k2tog, k16, k2tog tbl, k9, k2tog tbl, k1. *40 sts*

Row 42 K1, k2tog, k8, k2tog, k14, k2tog tbl, k8, k2tog tbl, k1. *36 sts*

Row 44 K1, k2tog, k7, k2tog, k12, k2tog tbl, k7, k2tog tbl, k1. *32 sts*

Row 46 K1, k2tog, k6, k2tog, k10, k2tog tbl, k6, k2tog tbl, k1. *28 sts*

Work as given for back from *** to end.

Ears (make 2)

Using yarn B and 3.75mm (US size 5) needles, cast on 4 sts.

Row 1 Knit.

Row 2 K1, M1, k2, M1, k1. *6 sts*

Row 3 K1, M1, p4, M1, k1. *8 sts*

Row 4 Knit.

Row 5 K1, M1, p6, M1, k1. *10 sts*

Row 6 Knit.

Row 7 K2, p6, k2.

Rows 8 to 13 As Rows 6 and 7, 3 times.

Row 14 K1, k2tog, k4, k2tog tbl, k1. *8 sts*

Row 15 K2, p4, k2.

Row 16 K1, k2tog, k2, k2tog tbl, k1. *6 sts*

Row 17 K1, k2tog, k2tog tbl, k1. *4 sts*

Cast off.

Eye patch

Using yarn B and 3.75mm (US size 5) needles, cast on 13 sts.

Row 1 K1, M1, k to last st, M1, k1. *15 sts*

Row 2 Purl.

Row 3 K1, M1, k to last st, M1, k1. *17 sts*

Beg with p row, work 3 rows in St st.

Row 7 K8, turn leaving rem 9 sts on holder.

**Next row Purl.

Next row K2tog, k to last 2 sts, k2tog tbl. *6 sts*

Next row Purl.

Next row K2tog, k to last 2 sts, k2tog tbl. *4 sts*

Cast off purlwise.

Rejoin yarn B to rem sts.

Next row Cast off 1 st, k to end. *8 sts*

Work as given for other side from **.

Muzzle

Using yarn B and 3.75mm (US size 5) needles, cast on 8 sts.

Row 1 Purl.

Row 2 K1, *M1, k2, rep from * to last st, M1, k1. *12 sts*

Purl next and every foll alt row.

Row 4 K3, *M1, k3, rep from * to end. *15 sts*

Row 6 K3, *M1, k3, rep from * to end. *19 sts*

Row 8 K2, *M1, k3, rep from * to last 2 sts, M1, k2. *25 sts*

Row 10 K2, *M1, k3, rep from * to last 2 sts, M1, k2. *33 sts*

Beg with p row, work 9 rows in St st.

Row 20 K1, k2tog, *k8, k2tog, rep from * to end. *29 sts*

Row 22 *K2tog, k1, rep from * to last 2 sts, k2tog. *19 sts*

Row 24 K1, *k2tog, rep from * to end. *10 sts*

Row 26 *K2tog, rep from * to end. *5 sts*

Row 27 P2tog, p1, p2tog tbl. *3 sts*

Break yarn and thread through rem 3 sts.

Pull up tight and fasten off securely.

Hands (make 2)

Using yarn B and 3.75mm (US size 5) needles, cast on 20 sts.

Row 1 Purl.

Row 2 K1, M1, k8, M1, k2, M1, k8, M1, k1. *24 sts*

Beg with p row, work 13 rows in St st.

Row 16 K1, k2tog, k6, k2tog tbl, k2, k2tog, k6, k2tog tbl, k1. *20 sts*

Row 17 Purl.

Row 18 K1, k2tog, k4, k2tog tbl, k2, k2tog, k4, k2tog tbl, k1. *16 sts*

Cast off.

Tail

Using yarn A and 2.75mm (US size 2) needles, cast on 100 sts.

Change to 3.75mm (US size 5) needles.

Beg with p row, work 10 rows in St st.

Change to 2.75mm (US size 2) needles.

Next row Purl.

Cast off.

Making up

Join front and back sections using mattress st, fill with toy stuffing as you go.

Fold cast-on edge of ears in half and sew in place on side seam of head, using the image as a guide.

With cast-on edge at the top, sew muzzle in place using the image as a guide and leaving a gap. Fill with toy stuffing and sew up the gap.

Sew the eye patch in position along the top edge of the muzzle using the image as a guide.

Fill the hands with toy stuffing and attach to the ends of the arms.

Using mattress st, sew together cast-on and cast-off edges of tail. Stuff firmly as you go along to create curl. Attach tail to monkey's bottom.

Using yarn A, stitch on eyes, mouth and nostrils, using image as a guide.

Scarves

There are three scarf styles to choose from: scarf A (below left) is in moss stitch, scarf B (below right) is stripy garter stitch and scarf C (opposite) is in Fairisle in stocking stitch.

Skill level

* to **

Scarf A: plain

Using an oddment of *Felted Tweed DK* (shown using 152 Watery) and 3.75mm (US size 5) needles, cast on 14 sts.

Row 1 *K1, p1, rep from * to end.
Row 2 *P1, k1, rep from * to end.
These 2 rows form moss st patt.
Cont in patt until scarf measures approx 65cm/25½in.
Cast off in patt.

Scarf B: striped

Using 2 different oddments of *Felted Tweed DK* or *Wool Cotton* (shown using *Felted Tweed DK* 152 Watery and 154 Ginger) and 3.75mm (US size 5) needles, cast on 14 sts.

Scarf A: plain

Scarf B: striped

cute little knits

Rows 1 and 2 Knit using one of chosen shades.
Rows 3 and 4 Knit using other chosen shade.
These 4 rows form garter st stripe patt.
Cont in patt until scarf measures approx 65cm/25½in.
Cast off.

Scarf C: Fairisle
Using 3 different yarns – shown using *Wool Cotton* 900 Antique (A) and *Felted Tweed DK*

152 Watery (B) and 154 Ginger (C) – and 3.75mm (US size 5) needles, cast on 30 sts. Working in St st throughout using the Fairisle technique (see page 61) and repeating the 22 row patt rep, work from chart until scarf measures approx 65cm/25½in, ending with a RS row.
Cast off.

Making up
With WS together fold in half lengthways to form a tube and join row end edges using mattress st.
Join cast-on edges using mattress st, ensuring long seam is at centre back.
Join cast-off edge in same way.

Scarf C: Fairisle

KEY
☐ A
☒ B
◤ C

lazy lace throw

This would make a lovely project for a relative novice wanting to knit a simple lace pattern. It has a 10-row pattern repeat and is made in panels, knitted in cosy Rowan *Kid Classic*. You could increase the size of the throw by adding panels and increasing the length of each, but remember to increase the yarn quantities accordingly.

Skill level
*

Finished size
Completed throw measures approx 90 x 120cm/35½ x 47¼in

Yarn
Rowan *Kid Classic*
6 x 50g/1½oz balls cream (828 Feather)

Needles
1 pair 5.5mm (US size 9) needles

Tension
15 sts and 20 rows to 10cm/4in square measured over patt using 5.5mm (US size 9) needles.

Abbreviations
See page 62.

Centre strip
Using 5.5mm (US size 9) needles, cast on 46 sts.
Row 1 K1, *yf, k2tog tbl, k3, rep from * to end.
Purl next and every foll alt row.

Row 3 K2, *yf, k2tog tbl, k3, rep from * to last 4 sts, yf, k2tog tbl, k2.

Row 5 K3, *yf, k2tog tbl, k3, rep from * to last 3 sts, yf, k2tog tbl, k1.

Row 7 K4, *yf, k2tog tbl, k3, rep from * to last 2 sts, yf, k2tog tbl.

Row 9 K5, *yf, k2tog tbl, k3, rep from * to last st, k1.

Row 10 Purl.

These 10 rows form patt.

Work a further 240 rows, ending with a WS row.

Cast off.

Left strip

Using 5.5mm (US size 9) needles, cast on 45 sts.

Row 1 *K3, k2tog, yf, rep from * to last 5 sts, k5.

Row 2 and every foll alt row K4, p to end.

Row 3 K2, k2tog, yf, *k3, k2tog, yf, rep from * to last 6 sts, k6.

Row 5 K1, k2tog, yf, *k3, k2tog, yf, rep from * to last 7 sts, k7.

Row 7 K2tog, yf, *k3, k2tog, yf, rep from * to last 8 sts, k8.

Row 9 K1, *k3, k2tog, yf, rep from * to last 9 sts, k9.

Row 10 As Row 2.

These 10 rows form patt.

Work a further 240 rows, ending with a WS row.

Cast off.

Right strip

Using 5.5mm (US size 9) needles, cast on 45 sts.

Row 1 K7, k2tog, yf, *k3, k2tog, yf, rep from * to last st, k1.

Row 2 and every foll alt row P to last 4 sts, k4.

Row 3 K6, k2tog, yf, *k3, k2tog, yf, rep from * to last 2 sts, k2.

Row 5 K5, k2tog, yf, *k3, k2tog, yf, rep from * to last 3 sts, k3.

Row 7 K4, k2tog, yf, *k3, k2tog, yf, rep from * to last 4 sts, k4.

Row 9 K5, *k3, k2tog, yf, rep from * to last 5 sts, k5.

Row 10 As Row 2.

These 10 rows form patt.

Work a further 240 rows, ending with a WS row.

Cast off.

Making up

Join left, centre and right strips using mattress st.

Borders (make 2)

Using 5.5mm (US size 9) needles, cast on 4 sts.

Work in garter st until border fits across cast-on/cast-off edge of throw.

Cast off.

Attach border using mattress st.

leaf hottie cover

This elegant large-scale leaf design is knitted using the intarsia technique (see page 61). It makes a great hot water bottle cover or a nightdress case. The back is also patterned, although you could knit it plain. Two buttons fasten the ribbed top opening.

Skill level
**

Finished size
Approx 21 x 37cm/8¼ x 14½in

Yarns
Rowan *Pure Wool DK*
A 2 x 50g/1½oz balls cream (013 Enamel)
B 1 x 50g/1½oz ball teal (007 Cypress)
C 1 x 50g/1½ oz ball light blue (006 Pier)
D 1 x 50g/1½oz ball dark green
     (023 Shamrock)
E 1 x 50g/1½oz ball olive (020 Parsley)

Needles
1 pair 4mm (US size 6) needles

Extras
Two x 25mm/1in buttons (Coats 1055)

Tension
22 sts and 30 rows to 10cm/4in square measured over St st using 4mm (US size 6) needles.

Abbreviations
See page 62.

Pattern notes
When working from chart, odd numbered rows are k rows and read from right to left. Even numbered rows are p rows and read from left to right.
This pattern uses the intarsia method of joining colours (see page 61).

Front

Using yarn A and 4mm (US size 6) needles, cast on 50 sts.

Beg and ending rows as indicated, using the intarsia method, now work 118 rows in patt from chart A, which is worked entirely in St st beg with a k row, ending with a WS row.

Cast off.

Back

Lower section

Using yarn A and 4mm (US size 6) needles, cast on 50 sts.

Row 1 K2, *p2, k2, rep from * to end.

Row 2 P2, *k2, p2, rep from * to end.

These two rows form rib.

Work in rib for a further 14 rows ending with a WS row.

Beg and ending rows as indicated, using the intarsia method, now work 74 rows in patt from chart B, which is worked entirely in St st beg with a k row, ending with a WS row.

Cast off.

Chart A

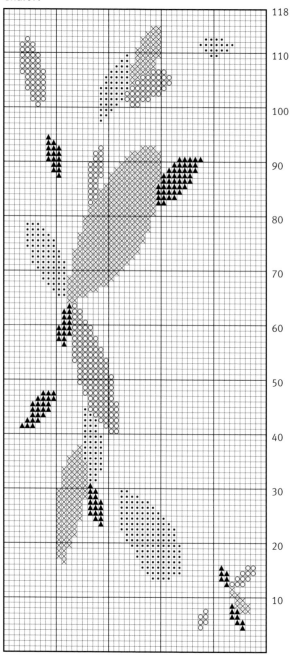

Jem says
If you want to create
a flowery version,
why not change the
blues and greens of
the leaves into petals,
using brighter shades,
such as pinks and
purples?

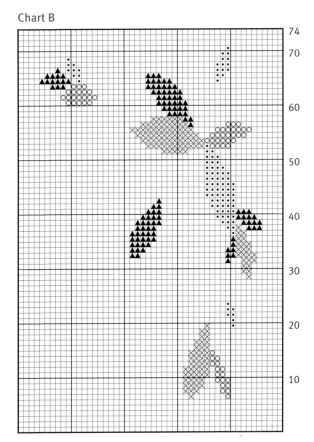

Chart C

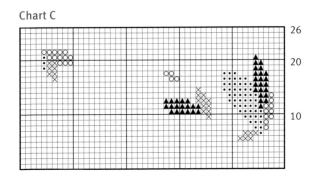

KEY

☐ A
☒ B
▲ C
◙ D
⊡ E

leaf hottie cover **31**

Upper section

Using yarn A and 4mm (US size 6) needles, cast on 50 sts.

Beg and ending rows as indicated, using the intarsia method, now work 26 rows in patt from chart C, which is worked entirely in St st beg with a k row, ending with a WS row.

Now work in rib as set on back lower section for 7 rows, ending with a RS row.

Make buttonhole on next 2 rows:

Next row (WS) [P2, k2] 3 times, cast off 4 sts, [p2, k2] 4 times, p2, cast off 4 sts, [k2, p2] 3 times.

Next row [K2, p2] 3 times, cast on 4 sts, [k2, p2] 4 times, k2, cast on 4 sts, [p2, k2] 3 times.

Work in rib for a further 7 rows.

Cast off in rib.

Making up

Using mattress st, join the cast-off edge of lower section of back to the cast-on edge of front section, then the cast-on edge of upper section of back to cast-off edge of front.

Join both side seams together allowing the rib of the top to overlap the rib of the bottom section.

Sew buttons in position to match the buttonholes.

bobble bath mat

This is a great project to test out your bobble-making skills. It is knitted in Rowan *Creative Focus Worsted*, which felts down beautifully, and is created with a central panel with the rows of bobbles, and borders which are stitched to the central panel. It comes in two sizes but remember that it is approximately one third larger before felting.

Skill level

*

Finished size

Small bath mat
Before felting: Bath mat measures approx 68 x 87cm/26¾ x 34¼in
After felting: Bath mat measures approx 42 x 52.5cm/16½ x 20¾in
Large bath mat
Before felting: Bath mat measures approx 119 x 153.5cm/46¾ x 60½in
After felting: Bath mat measures approx 73.5 x 92.5cm/29 x 36½in

Yarn

Rowan *Creative Focus Worsted*
4 (12) x 100g/3oz balls cream (100 Natural)

Needles

1 pair 5.5mm (US size 9) needles

Tension

16 sts and 30 rows to 10cm/4in square measured over bobble pattern using 5.5mm (US size 9) needles before felting.

Special abbreviations

MB – make bobble, (k1, p1, k1, p1, k1) all into next st, turn, k5, turn, p5, pass 2nd, 3rd, 4th and 5th sts over first st. 1 st remains and the bobble is complete. See also page 62.

Centre panel

Using 5.5mm (US size 9) needles, cast on 62 (126) sts.

Row 1 *K1, p1, rep from* to end.

Row 2 *P1, k1, rep from* to end.

These 2 rows form moss st border patt. Cont in patt for a further 32 rows ending with a WS row.

Row 35 Patt 6 (9), *M1, patt 8 (9), rep from * end. *69 (139) sts*

Rows 36 to 44 Knit.

Row 45 K6, *MB, k6, rep from * to end.

Rep the last 10 rows 18 (37) times more. *19 (38) rows of bobbles*

Knit 8 rows.

Next row K6 (9), * k2tog, k7 (8), rep from * to end. *62 (126) sts*

Work in moss st border patt for 35 rows. Cast off.

Side borders (both alike)

Using 5.5mm (US size 9) needles, cast on 20 sts. Place marker on last st.

Row 1 K2, *p1, k1, rep from * to end.

Row 2 *K1, p1, rep from * to last 2 sts, k2.

These 2 rows form moss st patt with first and last st knitted. Work a further 242 (404) rows, ending with a WS row. Cast off in patt.

Making up

With markers on the outside edge, attach side borders to the centre section using mattress st.

Felt bath mat in the washing machine on its own at 30°C/86°F.

See also page 62.

Jem says
If you want to create a colourful alternative, you could choose a brighter shade throughout or you could make the bobbles in a contrasting colour. Always ensure you run a test swatch through the washing machine before felting the final knitted piece.

cute little knits

bow slippers

These slippers are both cosy and smart. The uppers and bows are knitted in Rowan *Felted Tweed DK* and the lining and sole in Rowan *British Sheep Breeds Bouclé*, a naturally curly yarn. The soles are felted for durability.

Skill level
**

Finished size
Small/medium
24cm/9½in long
Medium/large
25.5cm/10in long

Yarns
Rowan *British Sheep Breeds Bouclé*
A 2 x 100g/3oz balls cream (220 Ecru)
Rowan *Felted Tweed DK*
B 1 x 50g/1½oz ball red (150 Rage)

Needles
1 pair 8mm (US size 11) needles
1 pair 3.75mm (US size 5) needles

Tension
8 sts and 12 rows to 10cm/4in square
measured over St st using 8mm (US size 11)
needles and yarn A.
24 sts and 32 rows to 10cm/4in square
measured over St st using 3.75mm (US size
5) needles and yarn B.

Abbreviations
See page 62.

Foot lining (both alike)
Using yarn A and 8mm (US size 11) needles,
cast on 3 sts.
Row 1 (WS) Purl.
Row 2 K1, M1, k to last st, M1, k1. *5 sts*
Rep last 2 rows 3 times more. *11 sts*
Beg with p row, work 8 (10) rows in St st.
Next row P5, turn leaving rem sts on a
holder.
Work each side of foot lining
separately.
Beg with k row, work 10 rows in St st.
Next row K4, M1, k1.
Beg with p row, work 9 rows in St st.

Cast off.

With WS facing, rejoin yarn to rem sts.

Next row Sl 1, p1, psso, p to end. *5 sts*

Beg with k row, work 10 rows in St st.

Next row K1, M1, k4.

Beg with p row, work 9 rows in St st.

Cast off.

Sole (both alike)

Using yarn A and 8mm (US size 11) needles, cast on 4 sts.

Row 1 (WS) Purl.

Row 2 K1, M1, k to last st, M1, k1. *6 sts*

Rep last 2 rows once more. *8 sts*

Beg with p row, work 33 (37) rows in St st.

Next row K1, k2tog, k to last 3 sts, k2tog tbl, k1. *6 sts*

Dec as set on foll alt row. *4 sts*

Cast off purlwise.

Foot (both alike)

Using yarn B and 3.75mm (US size 5) needles, cast on 7 sts.

Row 1 (WS) Purl.

Row 2 K1, M1, k to last st, M1, k1. *9 sts*

Rep last 2 rows 7 times more. *23 sts*

Next row Purl.

Next row K5, M1, k13, M1, k5. *25 sts*

Next row Purl.

Next row K5, M1, k15, M1, k5. *27 sts*

Beg with p row, work 3 (5) rows in St st.

Next row K5, M1, k17, M1, k5. *29 sts*

Beg with p row, work 3 (5) rows in St st.

Next row K5, M1, k19, M1, k5. *31 sts*

Beg with p row, work 3 (7) rows in St st.

Next row K5, M1, k21, M1, k5. *33 sts*

Next row Purl.

Next row K12, k2tog, k1, turn leaving rem sts on a holder. *14 sts*

Work each side of the foot separately.

Beg with a p row, work 19 rows in St st.

Next row K1, M1, k to end.

Rep last 4 rows twice more. *17 sts*

Beg with a p row, work 19 rows in St st.

Cast off.

With RS facing, rejoin yarn to rem sts.

Next row Cast off centre 3 sts, 1 st on right needle, k2tog tbl, k to end. *14 sts*

Beg with a p row, work 19 rows in St st.

Next row K to last st, M1, k1.

Rep last 4 rows twice more. *17 sts*

Beg with a p row, work 19 rows in St st.

Cast off.

Bow

Main section (both alike)

Using yarn B and 3.75mm (US size 5) needles, cast on 16 sts.

Row 1 *P1, k1, rep from * to end.

Row 2 *K1, p1, rep from * to end.

These 2 rows form moss st pattern, cont in moss st until strip measures 11cm/4¼in.

Cast off in patt.

Centre section (both alike)

Using yarn B and 3.75mm (US size 5) needles, cast on 7 sts.

Row 1 *P1, k1, rep from * to last st, p1.

Row 2 K1, *p1, k1, rep from * to end.

These 2 rows form rib pattern, cont in rib until strip measures 5cm/2in.
Cast off in patt.

Making up
Felt the soles by machine washing on their own at 30°C/86°F.

With WS of foot facing the RS of foot lining, join pieces together using back st or mattress st if preferred and leaving a small border of the lining showing.

Join the foot sections to the felted soles using picture as a guide.

Wrap bow centre around the main section and join cast-on and cast-off edges to form bow.

Attach bows to slippers using picture as a guide.

Jem says
Be careful when felting the sole of the slipper if you are using a different shade of the British Sheep Breeds Bouclé yarn, as the different colours come from different breeds of sheep and may felt differently.

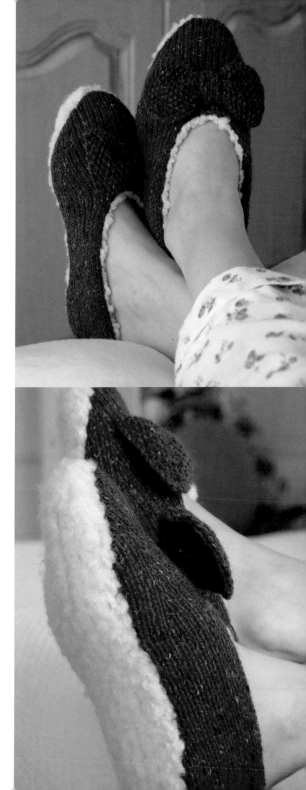

little hearts

These lovely hearts have two different but simple Fairisle designs, with a checkered or plain back, but you can mix and match them (for plain ones, just follow the shaping for the Front, ignoring chart). If you knit them using oddments of yarn, such as *Wool Cotton* or *Felted Tweed DK* (see front heart opposite), they will be slightly larger. The two other hearts opposite are in *Rowan Fine Tweed*. The centre one is 371 Wensley.

Skill level
**

Finished size
Finished heart measures approx 8 x 8cm/ 3¼ x 3¼in

Yarns
Rowan Fine Tweed
A 1 x 25g/¾oz ball cream (376 Bell Busk)
B 1 x 25g/¾oz ball red (369 Bainbridge)

Needles
1 pair 3mm (US size 2/3) needles

Extras
Washable toy stuffing
Approx 35cm/13¾in of 10mm/½in ribbon
(Coats double satin: 2621110 shade 00355 red and 00101 off-white)
Dried lavender (optional)

Tension
27 sts and 38 rows to 10cm/4in square measured over patt using 3mm (US size 2/3) needles.

Chart A

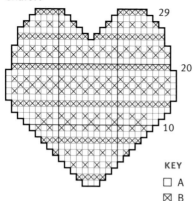

29
20
10

KEY

☐ A
☒ B

Chart B

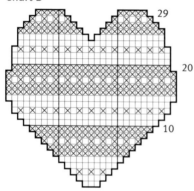

29
20
10

Chart C

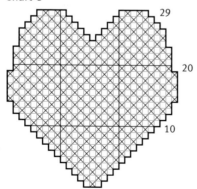

29
20
10

Abbreviations

See page 62.

Pattern notes

When working from chart, odd numbered rows are k rows and read from right to left. Even numbered rows are p rows and read from left to right.

This pattern uses the Fairisle method of joining colours (see page 61).

Front

Using yarn A and 3mm (US size 2/3) needles, cast on 3 sts.

Work from chart A or B, changing yarn colours as required, or as foll:

Starting with a k row and working in St st throughout, work from chart shaping heart as foll:

Row 1 Knit.

Row 2 P1, M1, p to last st, M1, p1. *5 sts*

Row 3 K1, M1, k to last st, M1, k1. *7 sts*

Rows 4 to 13 As Rows 2 and 3, 5 times. *27 sts*

Row 14 Purl.

Row 15 As Row 3. *29 sts*

Work 4 rows.

Row 20 P2tog, p to last 2 sts, p2tog tbl. *27 sts*

Work 3 rows.

Row 24 As Row 20. *25 sts*

Row 25 K12, turn leaving rem sts on a holder.

Work each side separately.

Row 26 P2tog, p to end. *11 sts*

Row 27 K2tog, k to last 2 sts, k2tog tbl. *9 sts*

Row 28 P2tog, p to last 2 sts, p2tog tbl. *7 sts*

Row 29 K2tog, k to last 2 sts, k2tog tbl. *5 sts*
Cast off.
With RS facing, rejoin yarn to rem sts.
Next row Cast off 1 st, k to end. *12 sts*
Work to match first side reversing shapings.
Cast off.

Back
Using yarn A and 3mm (US size 2/3)
needles, cast on 3 sts.

Work from chart C and shape as front.

Making up
With WS together, join front and back using
mattress st, leaving a small gap for stuffing
(plus optional lavender).
Once stuffed, complete joining. Thread
through ribbon and tie to form a loop.

little hearts

fantastic fox

This handsome fox with his big, bushy tail makes a great draught excluder in his larger size and a cute toy in the smaller one. He is knitted in two colours of Rowan *Felted Tweed DK*, with a little bit of Fairisle pattern on his tail.

Skill level
**

Finished size
Fox measures from nose to tip of tail:
Small toy: 81.5cm/32in
Draught excluder: 99cm/39in

Yarns
Rowan *Felted Tweed DK*
A 2 (2) x 50g/1½oz balls orange
    (154 Ginger)
B 1 (1) x 50g/1½oz ball cream (177 Clay)

Needles
1 pair 3.75mm (US size 5) needles

Extras

Washable toy filling

Three x 15mm/½in buttons for eyes and nose (Coats 0192)

Note: In a home with young children, replace buttons with embroidery.

Tension

23 sts and 32 rows to 10cm/4in square measured over St st using 3.75mm (US size 5) needles.

Abbreviations

See page 62.

Top section

Using yarn B and 3.75mm (US size 5) needles, cast on 3 sts.

Tail

Row 1 K1, *M1, k1, rep from * to end. 5 sts
Row 2 Purl.
Rep last 2 rows 3 times more. 33 sts
Row 9 K1, *M1, k2, rep from * to end. 49 sts
Row 10 Purl.
Row 11 K1, *M1, k3, rep from * to end. 65 sts
Row 12 Purl.
Row 13 K13, *M1, k13, rep from * to end.

69 sts

Beg with p row, work 11 (37) rows in St st.

Next row K1, k2tog, k to last 3 sts, k2tog tbl, k1. 67 sts

The last row sets dec.

Using the Fairisle technique (see page 61), work all 10 rows from chart, dec 1 st at each end of 4th and 1 foll 4th row as set by dec row. 63 sts

Cont in yarn A only dec 1 st at each end of 2nd and 15 foll 4th rows then 2 foll alt rows. 27 sts

Next row (WS) Purl.

Cast off 6 sts at beg of next 2 rows. 15 sts
Cast on 30 sts at end of next 2 rows. 75 sts

Back legs

Row 1 K20, M1, k17, M1, k1, M1, k17, M1, k20. 79 sts

Purl next and every foll alt row.

Row 3 K21, M1, k18, M1, k1, M1, k18, M1, k21. 83 sts

Row 5 K22, M1, k19, M1, k1, M1, k19, M1, k22. 87 sts

Row 7 K23, M1, k20, M1, k1, M1, k20, M1, k23. 91 sts

Row 9 K24, M1, k21, M1, k1, M1, k21, M1, k24. 95 sts

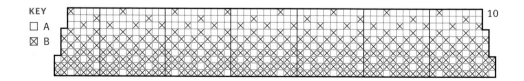

KEY
□ A
☒ B

10

Row 11 K25, M1, k22, M1, k1, M1, k22, M1, k25. *99 sts*

Row 13 K26, M1, k47, M1, k26. *101 sts*

Row 15 K27, M1, k23, M1, k1, M1, k23, M1, k27. *105 sts*

Row 17 K28, M1, k49, M1, k28. *107 sts*

Row 19 K29, M1, k24, M1, k1, M1, k24, M1, k29. *111 sts*

Cast off 28sts at beg of next 2 rows. *55 sts*

Beg with p row, work 41 (71) rows in St st.

Front legs

Cast on 28 sts at end of next 2 rows. *111 sts*

Row 1 K28, k2tog, k23, k2tog, k1, k2tog tbl, k23, k2tog tbl, k28. *107 sts*

Purl next and every foll alt row.

Row 3 K27, k2tog, k49, k2tog tbl, k27. *105 sts*

Row 5 K26, k2tog, k22, k2tog, k1, k2tog tbl, k22, k2tog tbl, k26. *101 sts*

Row 7 K25, k2tog, k47, k2tog tbl, k25. *99 sts*

Row 9 K24, k2tog, k21, k2tog, k1, k2tog tbl, k21, k2tog tbl, k24. *95 sts*

Row 11 K23, k2tog, k20, k2tog, k1, k2tog tbl, k20, k2tog tbl, k23. *91 sts*

Row 13 K22, k2tog, k19, k2tog, k1, k2tog tbl, k19, k2tog tbl, k22. *87 sts*

Row 15 K21, k2tog, k18, k2tog, k1, k2tog tbl, k18, k2tog tbl, k21. *83 sts*

Row 17 K20, k2tog, k17, k2tog, k1, k2tog tbl, k17, k2tog tbl, k20. *79 sts*

Row 19 K19, k2tog, k16, k2tog, k1, k2tog tbl, k16, k2tog tbl, k19. *75 sts*

Cast off 25 sts at beg of next 2 rows. *25 sts*

Jem says
For the knitted toy fox, why not add a scarf like the Fairisle one on page 23? You could use left over yarn in Felted Tweed from the fox in orange and cream, plus some oddments of blue Felted Tweed DK (152 Watery) from the scarf for the Monkey.

Head

Next row Purl.

Next row K12, M1, place marker, k1, place marker, M1, k12. *27 sts*

Inc by making 1 st before 1st marker and 1 st after 2nd marker on foll 5 alt rows and 3 foll 4th rows. *43 sts*

Beg with p row, work 5 rows in St st.

Next row K19, k2tog, (marker) k1, (marker) k2tog tbl, k19. *41 sts*

Dec 1 st before 1st marker and 1 st after 2nd marker as set by last row on 2 foll 6th rows then 3 foll 4th rows then 8 foll alt rows.

15 sts

Cast off.

Underside

Using yarn B and 3.75mm (US size 5)
needles, cast on 10 sts.
Beg with k row, work 10 rows in St st.

Back legs

Cast on 20 sts at end of next 2 rows. *50 sts*
Row 13 K20, M1, place marker, k10, place
marker, M1, k20. *52 sts*
Inc 1 st before 1st marker and 1 st after 2nd
marker on 9 foll alt rows. *70 sts*
Cast off 28sts at beg of foll 2 rows. *14 sts*
Beg with p row, work 41 (71) rows in St st.

Front legs

Cast on 28 sts at beg of next 2 rows. *70 sts*
Next row K28, k2tog, place marker, k10,
place marker, k2tog tbl, k28. *68 sts*
Dec 1 st before 1st marker and 1 st after 2nd
marker on 9 foll alt rows. *50 sts*
Cast off 20sts at beg of next 2 rows. *10 sts*
Beg with p row, work 57 rows in St st.
Next row K2tog, k to last 2 sts, k2tog tbl.
8 sts
Dec 1 st at each end of 3 foll 4th rows as set
by last row. *2 sts*
Break yarn and thread through rem 2 sts.
Fasten off securely.

Outer ears

Using yarn A and 3.75mm (US size 5)
needles, cast on 18 sts.
Row 1 Knit.
Purl next and every foll alt row.

Row 3 K7, k2tog, k2tog tbl, k7. *16 sts*
**Row 5 K6, k2tog, k2tog tbl, k6. *14 sts*
Row 7 K5, k2tog, k2tog tbl, k5. *12 sts*
Row 9 K4, k2tog, k2tog tbl, k4. *10 sts*
Row 11 K3, k2tog, k2tog tbl, k3. *8 sts*
Row 13 K2, k2tog, k2tog tbl, k2. *6 sts*
Row 15 K1, k2tog, k2tog tbl, k1. *4 sts*
Row 17 K2tog, k2tog tbl. *2 sts*
Break yarn and thread through rem 2 sts.
Fasten off securely.

Inner ears
Using yarn B and 3.75mm (US size 5)
needles, cast on 16 sts.
Row 1 Knit.

Purl next and every foll alt row.
Work as outer ear from **.

Making up
Fold cast-off edge of top section in half and
join to form nose.
Join tail seam using mattress st, filling with
toy stuffing as you go.
Join underbelly to top section using mattress
st, filling with toy stuffing as you go.
Stitch inner ears to outer ears using mattress
st then attach to head using image as a guide.
Using yarn A, sew on buttons for eyes and
nose using image as a guide.

fantastic fox

birdie cosies

This group of designs features little birds in slightly different forms, knitted in *Rowan Fine Tweed* using Fairisle and intarsia techniques. The egg cup and mug cosy are the easiest. All three make a good introduction to colourwork.

tea cosy

Skill level
* to **

Finished size
Completed tea cosy measures approx 20cm/7¾in across the bottom, 8cm/3¼in across the top and 20cm/7¾in from top to bottom

Yarns
Rowan Fine Tweed
A 2 x 25g/¾oz balls green (371 Wensley)
B 1 x 25g/¾oz ball cream (376 Bell Busk)
C 1 x 25g/¾oz ball beige (360 Arncliffe)
D 1 x 25g/¾oz ball yellow (383 Leyburn)

Needles
1 pair 3.25mm (US size 3) needles

Extras
Five x 18mm/¾in buttons (Coats 0517)

Tension
26.5 sts and 38 rows to 10cm/4in square measured over St st using 3.25mm (US size 3) needles.

Abbreviations
See page 62.

Front
Using yarn A and 3.25mm (US size 3) needles, cast on 64 sts.
Row 1 *K1, p1, rep from * to end.
Row 2 *P1, k1, rep from * to end.
Rows 1 and 2 form moss st border. Work in moss st for a further 2 rows.
Row 5 [P1, k1] twice, cast off 3 sts, 1 st on right needle, [k1, p1] 4 times, k to last 4 sts,

KEY
- ☐ A
- ☒ B
- ▲ C
- ◲ D

Chart A

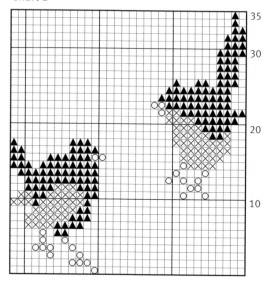

[p1, k1] twice.

Row 6 K1, p1, k1, p to last 13 sts, [k1, p1] 4 times, k1, cast on 3 sts, [k1, p1] twice.

Row 7 [P1, k1] 8 times, p1, k to last 4 sts, [p1, k1] twice.

Row 8 [K1, p1] twice, p to last 17 sts, p1, [k1, p1] 8 times.

Rep last 2 rows twice more.

Row 13 Cast off 13 sts, [k1, p1] twice, k to last 4 sts, [p1, k1] twice. *51 sts*

Row 14 K1, p1, k1, p to last 3 sts, k1, p1, k1.

Row 15 [K1, p1] twice, k to last 4 sts, [p1, k1] twice.

Rows 14 and 15 form main patt of St st with moss st edge.

Work 13 rows.

Chart B

Place chart

Next row Patt 5, work Row 1 of chart A, patt to end.

Next row Patt 4, work Row 2 of chart A, patt to end.

The last 2 rows set placement of chart. Cont as set until all 21 rows of chart have been worked.

Work a further 26 rows in main patt.

cute little knits

Row 76 K1, *p1, k1, rep from * to
end.
Rep last row twice more.
Cast off in moss st.

Back

Using yarn A and 3.25mm (US size 3)
needles, cast on 51 sts.
Row 1 K1, *p1, k1, rep from * to end.
Row 1 forms moss st border. Work in moss st
for a further 3 rows.
Row 5 [K1, p1] twice, k to last 4 sts, [p1, k1]
twice.
Row 6 K1, p1, k1, p to last 3 sts, k1, p1, k1.
Rows 5 and 6 form main patt of St st with
moss st edge.
Work 14 rows.

Place chart

Next row Patt 10, work Row 1 of chart B, patt
to end.
Next row Patt 9, work Row 2 of chart B, patt
to end.
The last 2 rows set placement of chart. Cont
as set until all 35 rows of chart have been
worked.
Work a further 20 rows in main patt.
Row 76 K1, *p1, k1, rep from * to
end.
Rep last row twice more.
Cast off in moss st.

*Jem says
If you want something that
looks bolder, then knit these
projects in Wool Cotton
4ply or Pure Wool 4ply,
both of which knit to a
similar tension.*

Making up

Place front section against your teapot and
place pins to mark the position of the top
and bottom of the spout on the LH side.
Place a pin to mark the top of the handle on
the RH side.
Lay front section on top of back section
with WS facing. Sew together down LH side
to first pin. Leave divide for spout. Sew
together from the second pin to the bottom
edge.
Sew together down RH side from top to pin.
Join top of left seam to the top of the right
seam then lay flat creating pleats. Pull
together top edge by sewing through both
layers and stitching a button on each side at
both edges.
Sew button on the bottom of back section to
match buttonhole strip under the handle.

egg cosy

Skill level
* to **

Finished size
Completed egg cosy measures approx
9 x 8cm/3½ x 3¼in

Yarns
Rowan Fine Tweed
A 1 x 25g/¾oz ball green (371 Wensley)
B 1 x 25g/¾oz ball cream (376 Bell Busk)
C 1 x 25g/¾oz ball beige (360 Arncliffe)
D 1 x 25g/¾oz ball yellow (383 Leyburn)

Needles
1 pair 3.25mm (US size 3) needles

Tension
26.5 sts and 38 rows to 10cm/4in square
measured over St st using 3.25mm (US size
3) needles.

Egg cosy
Using yarn A and 3.25mm (US size 3)
needles, cast on 45 sts.
Row 1 *K1, p1, rep from * to last st, k1.
Row 1 forms moss st border. Work in moss st
for a further 3 rows.
Now work in St st throughout.
Work 4 rows.

Place chart
Next row K5, work Row 1 of chart, k to end.
Next row P5, work Row 2 of chart, p to end.
The last 2 rows set placement of chart. Cont
as set until all 25 rows of chart have been
worked.
Work 3 rows.
Cast off.

Making up
Using mattress st, fold egg cosy in half and
join side and top seam.

KEY
☐ A
☒ B
▲ C
◖ D

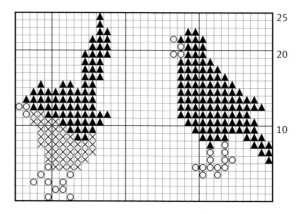

cute little knits

mug hug

Skill level
* to **

Finished size
Completed mug hug measures approx
18.5 x 7.5cm/7¼ x 3in

Yarns
Rowan Fine Tweed
A 1 x 25g/¾oz ball green (371 Wensley)
B 1 x 25g/¾oz ball cream (376 Bell Busk)
C 1 x 25g/¾oz ball beige (360 Arncliffe)
D 1 x 25g/¾oz ball yellow (383 Leyburn)

Needles
1 pair 3.25mm (US size 3) needles
3mm (US size C2/D3) crochet hook

Extras
Two x 18mm/¾in buttons (Coats 0517)

Tension
26.5 sts and 38 rows to 10cm/4in square
measured over St st using 3.25mm (US size
3) needles.

Mug hug
Using yarn A and 3.25mm (US size 3)
needles, cast on 52 sts.
Row 1 *K1, p1, rep from * to end.
Row 2 *P1, k1, rep from * to end.
Rows 1 and 2 form moss st border. Work in

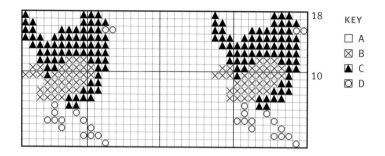

KEY

☐ A
☒ B
▲ C
◯ D

moss st for a further 2 rows.

Row 5 [K1, p1] twice, k to last 3 sts, p1, k1, p1.

Row 6 [P1, k1] twice, p to last 3 sts, k1, p1, k1.

Rows 5 and 6 form main patt of St st with moss st edge.

Cont in patt placing chart as foll:

Place chart

Next row Patt 6, work Row 1 of chart, patt to end.

Next row Patt 7, work Row 2 of chart, patt to end.

The last 2 rows set placement of chart. Cont as set until all 18 rows of chart have been worked.

Work a further 2 rows in main patt.

Work in moss st as set for border for 4 rows.

Cast off in moss st.

Button loops (both alike)

Using yarn A and 3mm (US size C2/D3) crochet hook, slip st into top RH corner and work a length of chain 8cm/3¼in (or length required for your mug). Slip st back into same place at top RH corner.

Make second loop in same way in bottom RH corner.

Making up

Sew one button at the top LH corner of mug hug and one at the bottom LH corner to correspond with button loops.

knitting know-how

Colourwork

There are two main methods of working with colour in knitted fabrics: the intarsia and the Fairisle techniques. The first method produces a single thickness of fabric and is usually used where a new colour is required for a block of stitches and rows in a particular area of a piece of knitting.

Where a small repeating colour pattern of up to 3 or 4 stitches is created across the row, the Fairisle technique is generally used.

Intarsia

In the intarsia technique, you have to join in a new yarn colour for each new block of colour stitches. To prevent the yarns getting twisted on the ball, the simplest method is to make individual little balls of yarn, or bobbins, from pre-cut short lengths of yarn, one for each motif or block of colour used in a row. You then work across the stitches, joining in the colours as required, by twisting them around each other where they meet on the wrong side of the work, to avoid gaps. After you have completed the piece of knitting, you need to neaten up the loose ends. They can either be darned along the colour joins or they can be knitted in to the fabric as each colour is worked by picking up the loops of the yarns carried across the back of the work as you knit.

Fairisle

When you are working a pattern with two or more repeating colours in the same row, you need to strand the yarn not in use behind the stitches being worked. This needs to be done with care, loosely enough to ensure that the strands not in use do not tighten and pucker the front of the knitting. To do this you need to treat the yarns not in use, known as 'floating yarns', as if they were one yarn and spread the stitches as you work to their correct width to keep them elastic. If your pattern demands that the stranded or floating yarns are carried across more than three stitches, it is wise to weave the new yarn colour under and over the colour yarn you are working with each time you change colours (over the first time, under the second time and so on). The alternating 'under and over' movement helps to prevent the floating yarns from tangling by keeping them caught at the back of the work.

It is important when knitting with more than one colour to keep your tension correct, as it easy to pull the loops of yarn too tight, puckering the work. If you tend to knit colourwork too tightly, increase your needle size for the colourwork section.

Finishing methods

Pressing

Block out each piece of knitting by pinning it on a board to the correct measurements in the pattern. Then lightly press it according to the ball band instructions, omitting any ribbed areas.

Take special care to press the edges as this makes sewing up easier and neater. If you cannot press the fabric, then cover the knitted fabric with a damp cloth and allow it to stand for a couple of hours.

Darn in all ends neatly along the selvedge edge or a colour join, as appropriate.

Stitching seams

When you stitch the pieces together, remember to match any areas of colour and texture carefully where they meet. Use a special seam stitch, called mattress stitch (in which you pick up a small stitch from the edge of each seam to be joined), as it creates the flattest seam. After all the seams are complete, press the seams and hems.

Lastly, sew on any buttons to correspond with the positions of any buttonholes.

Abbreviations

alt	alternate
approx	approximate
beg	begin(s)(ning)
cm	centimetres
cont	continu(e)(ing)
dec	decreas(e)(ing)
foll	follow(s)(ing)
garter st	garter stitch (K every row)
in	inch(es)
inc	increas(e)(ing)
K	knit
k2tog	knit next 2 stitches together
LH	left hand
m	metre(s)
M1	make one stitch by picking up horizontal loop before next stitch and knitting into back of it
M1P	make one stitch by picking up horizontal loop before next stitch and purling into back of it
mm	millimetres
P	purl
patt	pattern
psso	pass slipped stitch over
p2sso	pass two slipped stitches over
p2tog	purl next 2 stitches together
rem	remain(s)(ing)
rep	repeat
rev St st	reverse stocking stitch
RH	right hand
RS	right side
sl 1	slip one stitch
st(s)	stitch(es)
St st	stocking stitch (1 row K, 1 row P)
tbl	through back of loop(s)
tog	together
WS	wrong side
yd	yard(s)
yf	yarn forward

yarn information

The following Rowan yarns are specified in the patterns in this book. For *Felted Tweed DK*, you can substitute *Rowan Tweed,* which knits very much to the same specifications.

British Sheep Breeds Bouclé

A 100 per cent pure wool; 100g (60m/66yd) per ball. Recommended tension: 8.5 sts and 13 rows to 10cm/4in using 8mm (US size 11) knitting needles.

Creative Focus Worsted

A pure wool mix (75 per cent wool, 25 per cent alpaca); 100g (approximately 200m/220yd) per ball. Recommended tension: 20 sts and 24 rows to 10cm/4in using 4.5mm (US size 7) knitting needles.

Felted Tweed DK

A wool-alpaca-viscose mix (50 per cent merino wool, 25 per cent alpaca wool, 25 per cent viscose); 50g (approximately 175m/191yd) per ball. Recommended tension: 22–24 sts and 30–32 rows to 10cm/4in using 3.75–4mm (US size 5–6) knitting needles.

Kid Classic

A lambswool-mohair-polyamide mix yarn (70 per cent lambswool, 25 per cent kid mohair, 4 per cent polyamide); 50g (140m/153yd) per ball. Recommended tension: 18–19 sts and 23–25 rows to 10cm/4in using 5–5.5mm (US size 8–9) knitting needles.

Pure Wool DK

Machine washable 100 per cent pure wool; 50g (approximately 125m/137yd) per ball. Recommended tension 22 sts and 30 rows to 10cm/4in using 4mm (US size 6) knitting needles.

Rowan Fine Tweed

A 100 per cent pure wool; 25g (approximately 90m/98yd) per ball. Recommended tension: 26.5 sts and 38 rows to 10cm/4in using 3.25mm (US size 3) knitting needles.

Wool Cotton

A wool/cotton blend yarn (50 per cent merino wool, 50 per cent cotton); 50g (approximately 113m/123yd) per ball. Recommended tension: 22–24sts and 30–32 rows to 10cm/4in using 3.75–4mm (US size 5–6) knitting needles.

rowan yarn distributors

UK
Rowan, Green Lane Mill, Holmfirth,
West Yorkshire, HD9 2DX
Tel: +44 (0) 1484 681881
www.knitrowan.com

USA
Westminster Fibers Inc,
South Carolina, 29650
Tel: (800) 445-9276
www.westminsterfibers.com

AUSTRALIA
Australian Country Spinners Pty Ltd,
Melbourne 3004.
Tel: 03 9380 3830
Email: tkohut@auspinners.com.au

BENELUX
Coats Benelux, Ninove, 9400
Tel: 00 32 54 318989
Email: sales.coatsninove@coats.com

CANADA
See USA

CHINA
Coats Shanghai Ltd, Shanghai
Tel: 86 21 5774 3733
Email: victor.li@coats.com

DENMARK
Coats HP A/S, Copenhagen
Tel: 45 35 86 90 49
www.coatscrafts.dk

FINLAND
Coats Opti Crafts Oy, Kerava, 04220
Tel: (358) 9 274871
wwwcoatscrafts.fi

FRANCE
Coats Steiner, Mehun-Sur-Yèvre, 18500
Tel: 02 48 23 12 30
www.coatscrafts.fr

GERMANY
Coats GmbH, Kenzingen, 79341
Tel: 07162-14346
www.coatsgmbh.de

HONG KONG
See China

ICELAND
Rowan At Storkurinn, Reykjavik, 101
Tel: 551 8258
www.storkurinn.is

ISRAEL
Beit Hasidkit, Kfar Sava, 44256
Tel: (972) 9 7482381

ITALY
Coats Cucirini srl, Milano, 20126
Tel: (02) 636151
www.coatscucirini.com

KOREA
Coats Korea Co. Lt, Seoul, 137-060
Tel: 82-2-521-6262
www.coatskorea.co.kr

NEW ZEALAND
ACS New Zealand, Christchurch
Tel: 64-3-323-6665

NORWAY
Coats Knappehuset AS, Bergen, 5873
Tel: 55 53 93 00

PORTUGAL
Coats & Clark, Vila Nova de Gaia 4431-968
Tel: 223770700
www.crafts.com.pt

SINGAPORE
Golden Dragon Store, Singapore
Tel: (65) 65358454/65358234
Email: gdscraft@hotmail.com

SOUTH AFRICA
Arthur Bales Ltd, Johannesburg, 2195
Tel: (27) 118 882 401
www.arthurbales.co.za

SPAIN
Coats Fabra, Barcelona, 08030
Tel: (34) 93 290 84 00
www.coatscrafts.es

SWEDEN
Coats Expotex AB, Goteborg, 431 30
Tel: (46) 33 720 79 00
www.coatscrafts.se

SWITZERLAND
Coats Stroppel AG, Turgi (AG), CH-5300
Tel: 056 298 12 20
www.coatscrafts.ch

TAIWAN
Cactus Quality Co Ltd, Taiwan, R.O.C. 10084
Tel: 00886-2-23656527
www.excelcraft.com.tw

For stockists in all other countries please
contact Rowan for details

acknowledgements

Thanks to Susan, Anne and Lisa for all their work on the book. Rosie and Steve for
photography (and JJ Locations for interior photography location). Steph, Amy and both
Sophies for knitting little hearts and general encouragement. Rebecka for help with
technology! Sharon, Kate, David and all at Rowan for their support.

cute little knits